A year from now, you'll be glad you started today.

Savings Challenge Planner 2022-2023

Dede Sooyoo

ISBN 978-1-7330288-3-7(Paperback)

Dede Sooyoo LLC
P.O. Box 10866
Silver Spring, MD20914

Pearls of wisdom

Beginning of the savings journey, remember these pieces of advice:

- Be kind to yourself
- Savings journey is a marathon
- Enjoy the challenges
- Save your windfalls
- Be consistent
- When you go through a diversion ,you can still back on course.

Introduction

"Do something today that your future self will thank you for"
-@GustoNYC

The savings challenge planner intends to help cultivate great savings habits whiles having doing so.

There are five challenges in this planner, out of which two are customizable to your income
level or budget. You would find a tracker for each challenge, notes section, and motivational quotes to inspire you on your savings journey.

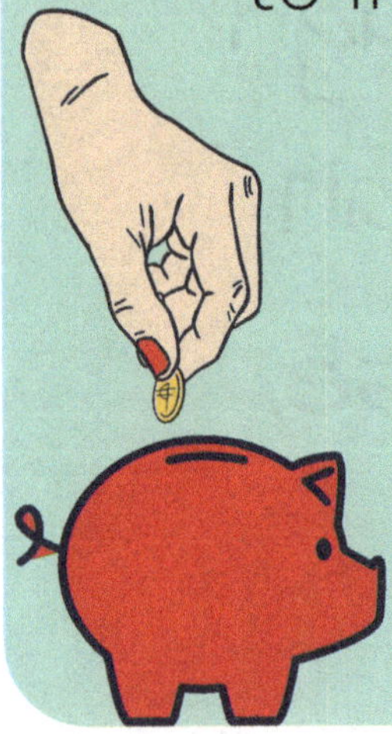

Begin your savings journey....

Table of Contents

#Twisted 52

"If you're saving, you're succeeding"
-Steve Bunkholder

Instructions: Select a number from 1-20. Be cautious and not choose a high number. You multiply by the number of weeks.

*** This is a customizable challenge*

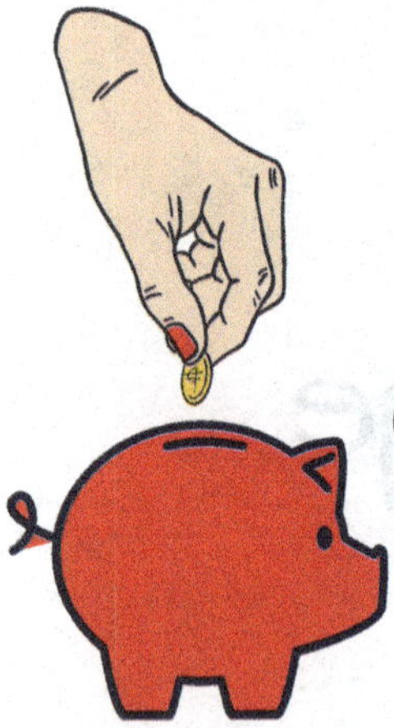

Begin your savings journey....

Best of Luck.

#Twisted 52

Weeks 1-18

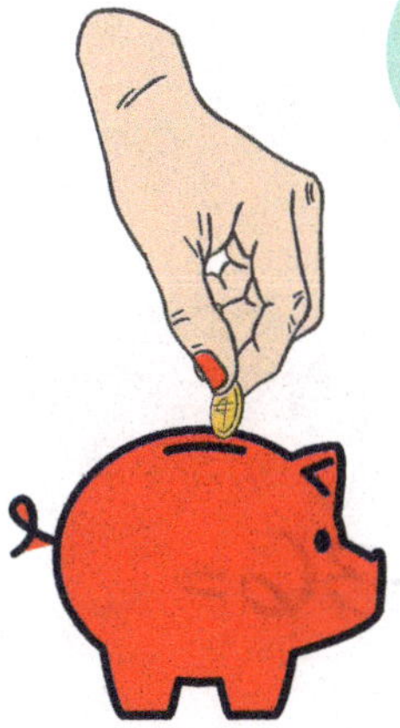

Totals for weeks 1-18=

#Twisted 52

Weeks 19-36

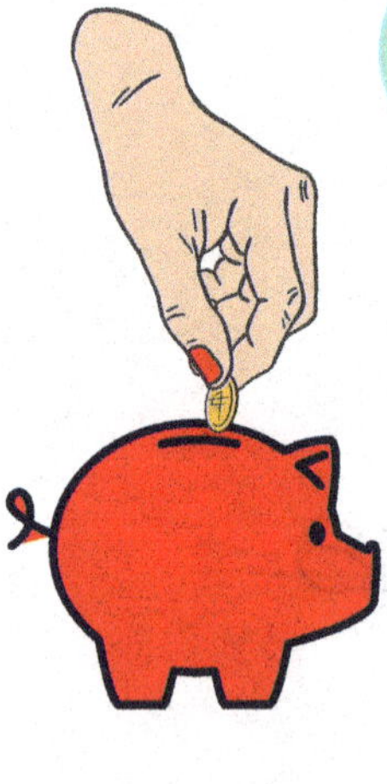

Totals for weeks 19-36=

#Twisted 52

Weeksl 37-52

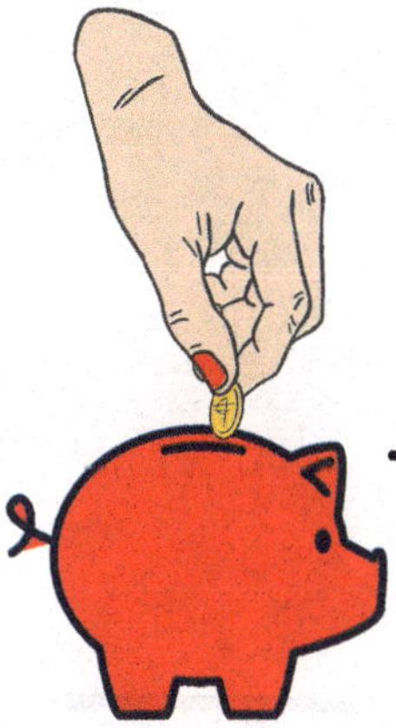

Totals for weeks 37-52=

Savings Tracker

Jan

Feb

Jul

Aug

Mar

Apr

Sep

Oct

May

Jun

Nov

Dec

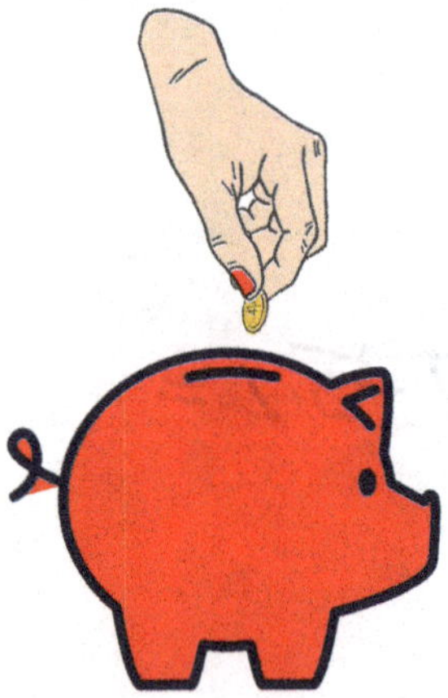

Total for the year= ________

Notes

Notes

Notes

Notes

Notes

Congratulations!!!!

You have completed a challenge.

You ready for the next?

Il believe in you...

The Say Hello to 2022

"It is great wealth to a soul
to live with a contented mind" -
Lucretius

Instructions

This challenge has to do with saving 25 .00 (in your local currency) 50 times in the the year..

Put with a ✔ or "X" in the circle the represents
25.00

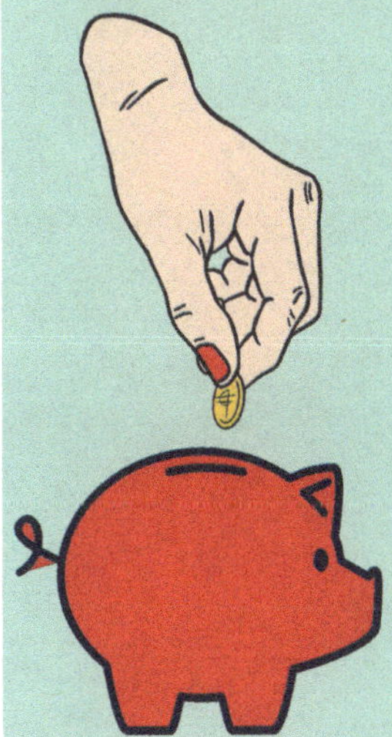

Begin your savings journey....

The Say Hello to 2022

BEGIN: **END:**

The Say Hello to 2022

BEGIN: **END:**

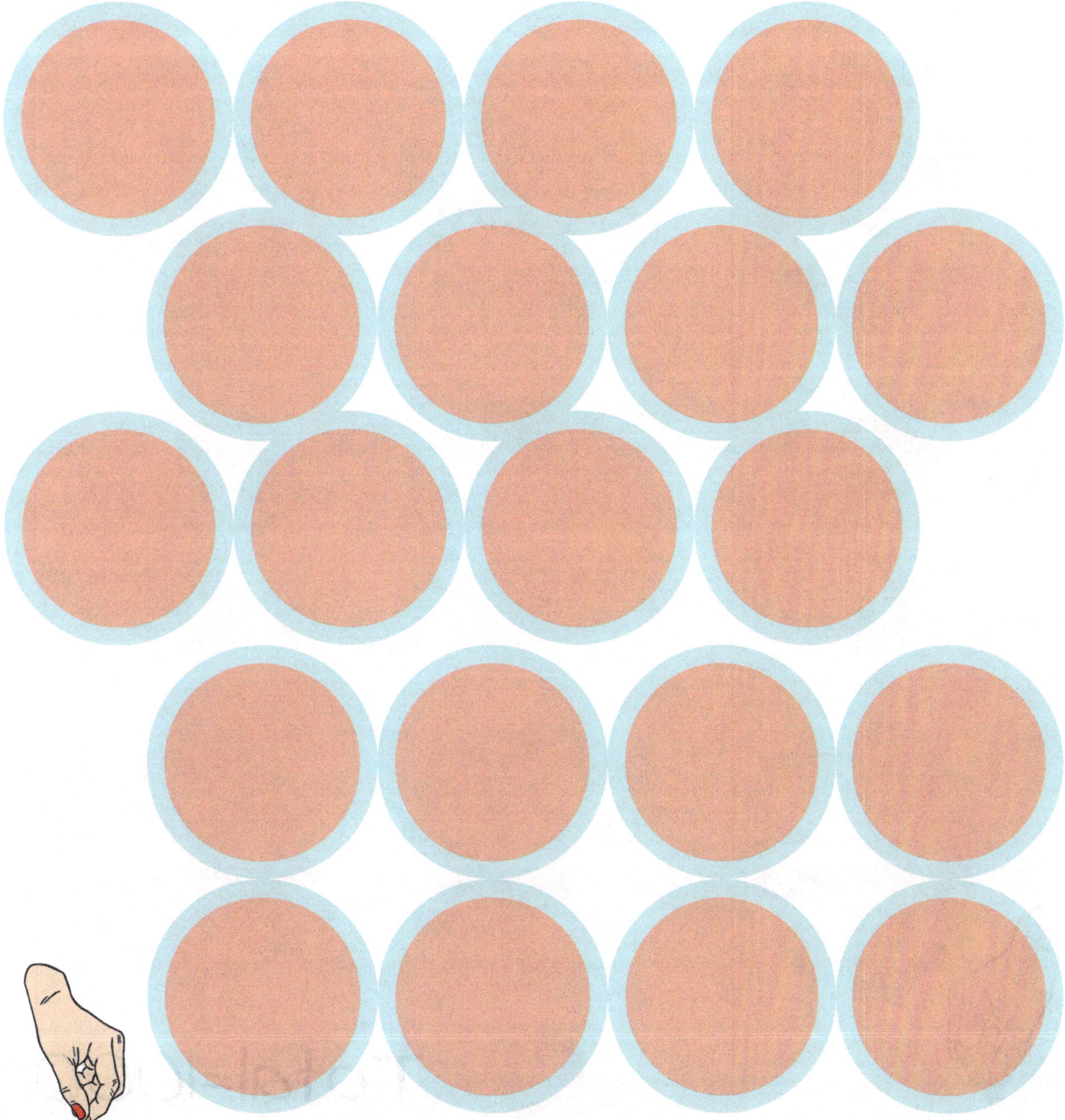

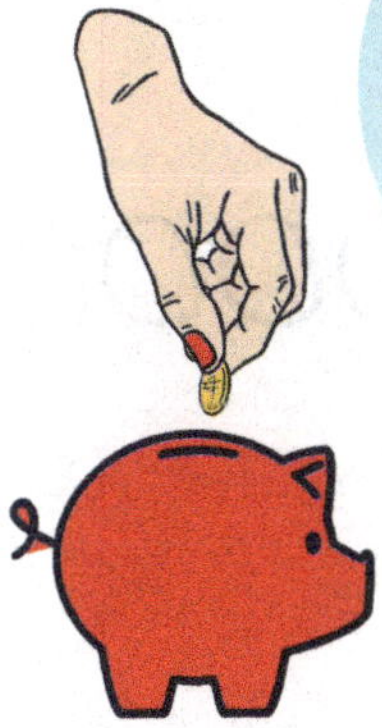

The Say Hello to 2022

BEGIN: **END:**

Total=1000

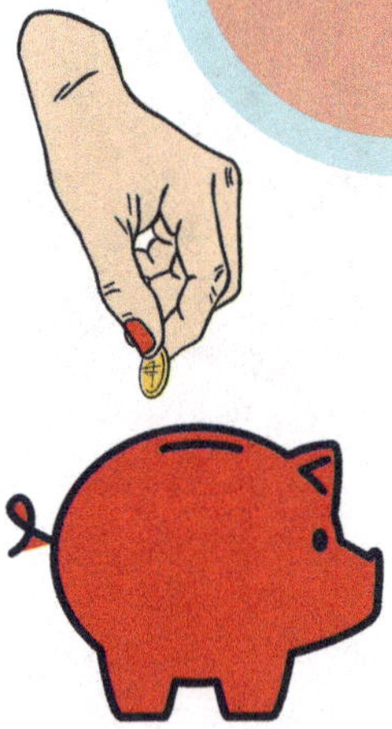

Savings Tracker

Jan

Feb

Mar

Apr

May

Jun

Jul

Aug

Sep

Oct

Nov

Dec

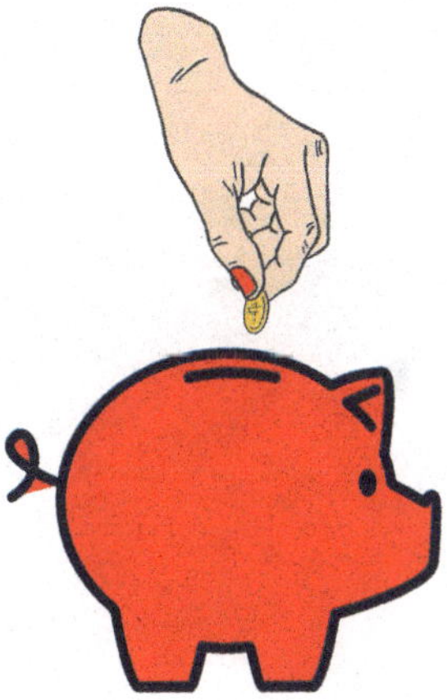

Total for the year= ________

Notes

Notes

Notes

Notes

Notes

Congratulations!!!!....

You have completed a challenge.

You ready for the next?

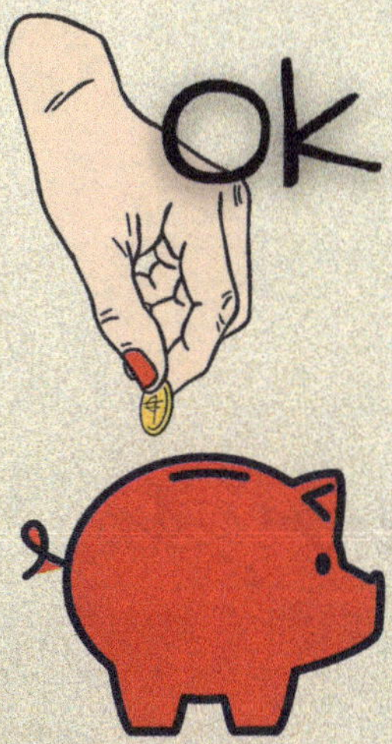

Ok Champ! Let's do this.

The 2023 FunTime

"A simple fact that is hard to learn is that the time to save money is when you have
you have some" - Joe Moore

Instructions

33.00(in your local currency) is represented by a bag of money. Use a ✔ when you have 33.00

Begin your savings journey....

The 2023 FunTime

BEGIN: END:

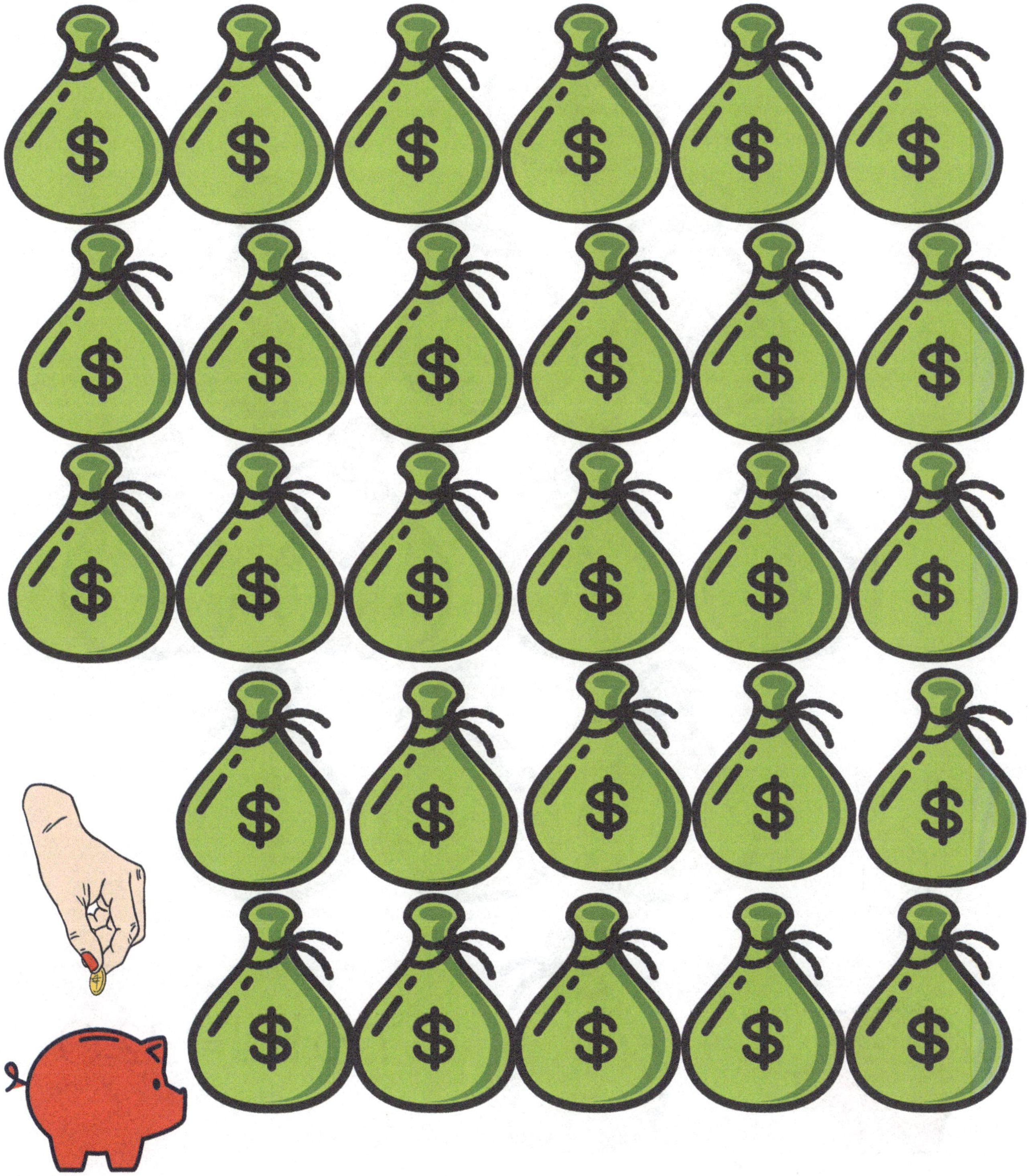

The 2023 FunTime

BEGIN: END:

Total=1320

Savings Tracker

Jan

Feb

Mar

Apr

May

Jun

Jul

Aug

Sep

Oct

Nov

Dec

Total for the year=. ________

Notes

Notes

Notes

Notes

Notes

Congratulations!!!!

You have completed a challenge.

You ready for the next?

Half of the journey,

Power forward!

Fund

"A fool can earn money, but it takes a wise man to save and dispose of it to his own advantage"- Brigham Young

Instructions

An emergency fund is something everyone needs to set up in their financial journey. In light of this, the amount every person needs to save varies.

Divide your desired amount by 100 days and write the amounts in the boxes.

**This is a customizable challenge

Begin your savings journey...

Fund

BEGIN: END:

AMOUNT:

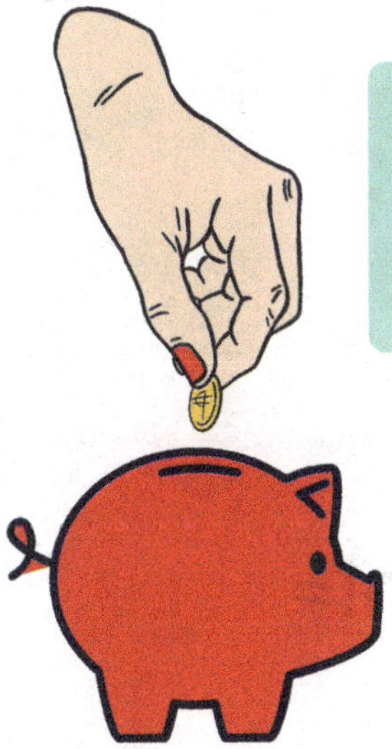

Total=

Fund

BEGIN: END:

AMOUNT:

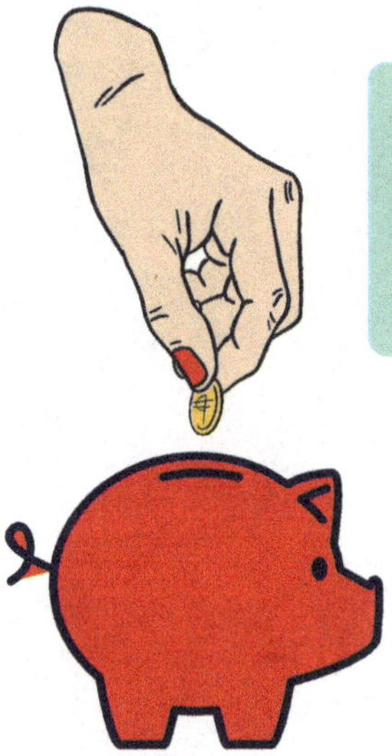

Total=

Fund

BEGIN: END:

AMOUNT:

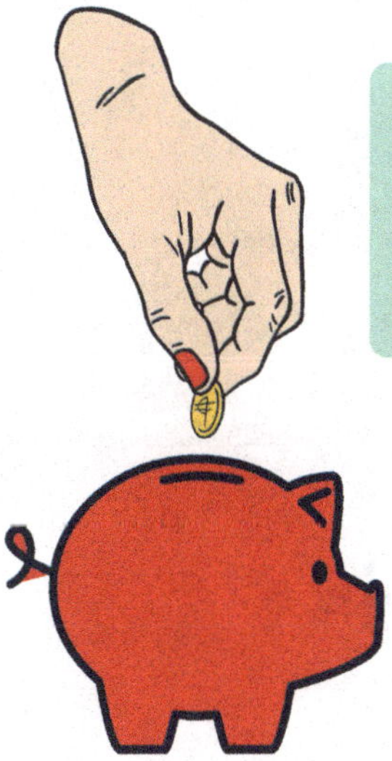

Total=

Fund

BEGIN: END:

AMOUNT:

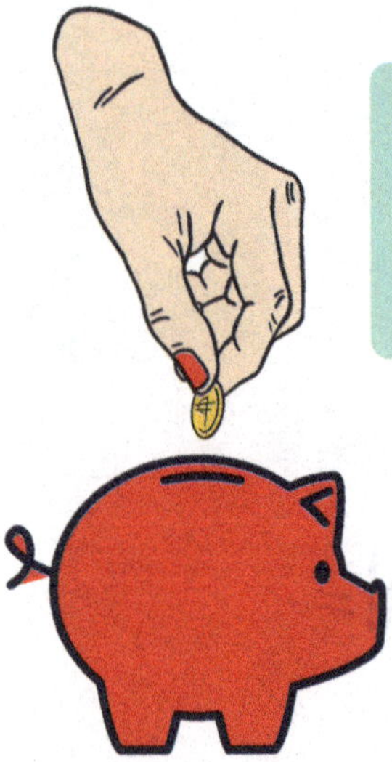

Total=

Fund

BEGIN: **END:**

AMOUNT:

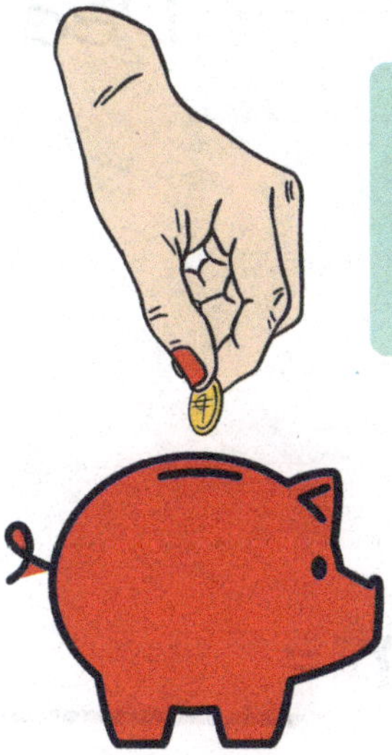

Total=

Savings Tracker

Jan

Feb

Mar

Apr

May

Jun

Jul

Aug

Sep

Oct

Nov

Dec

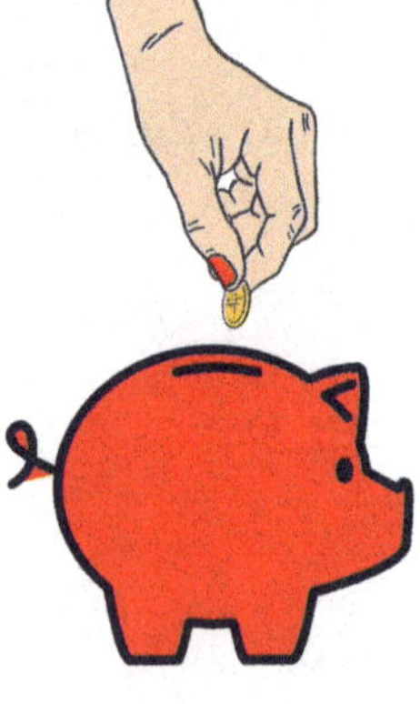

Total for the year=. ______

Notes

Notes

Notes

Notes

Notes

Congratulations!!!!

You have completed a challenge.

You ready for the next?

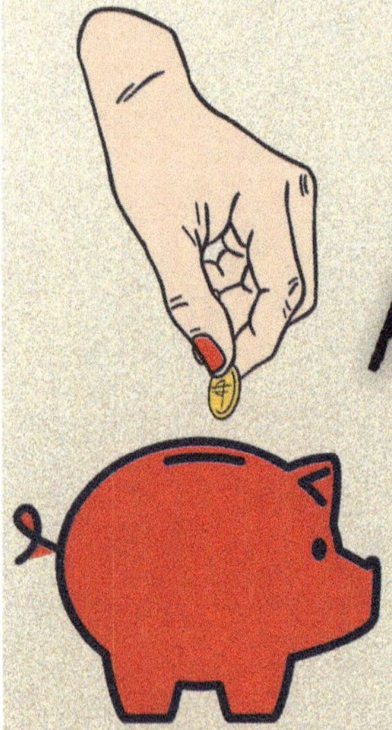

Almost there !!!

5260 challenge

"Do not save what is left after spending, but spend what is left after saving"
-Warren Buffet

Instructions

1 gold leaf = 52.60. Collect all 100 gold leaves by "X" and you would have successfully completed the final challenge. Be honest with yourself.

Begin your savings journey....

5260 challenge

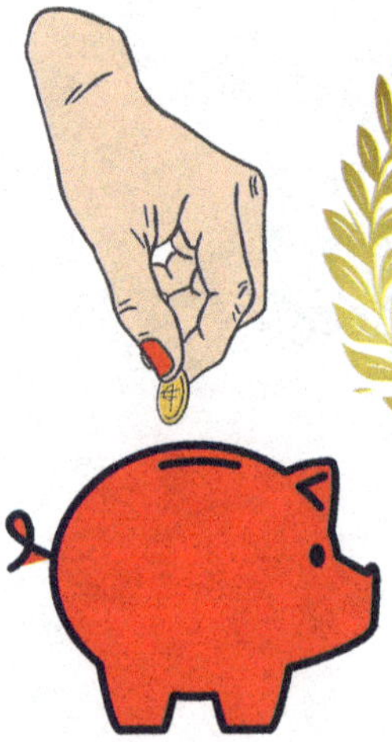

5260 challenge

5260 challenge

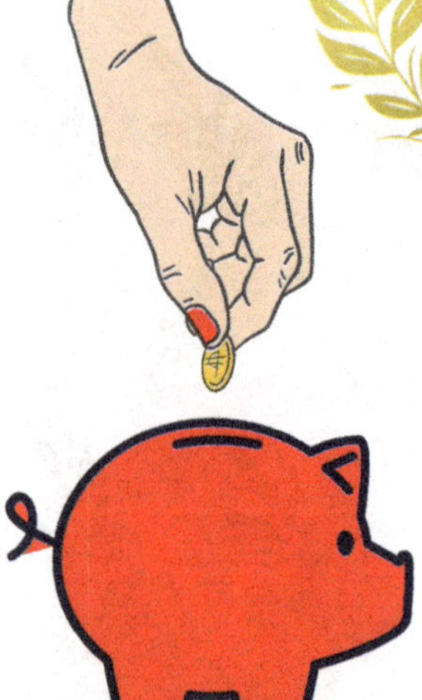

Total=5260

Savings Tracker

Jan

Feb

Mar

Apr

May

Jun

Jul

Aug

Sep

Oct

Nov

Dec

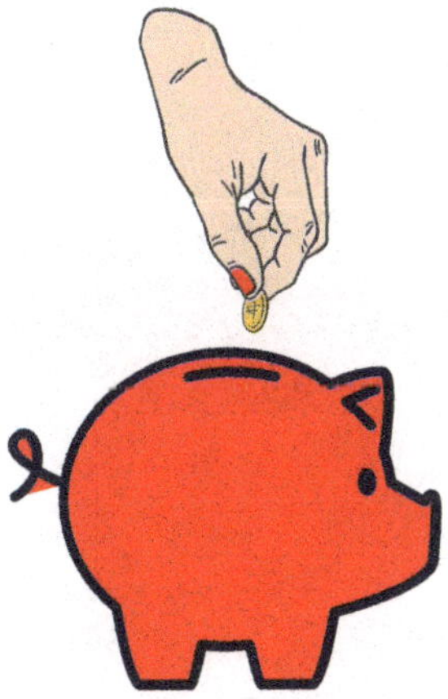

Total for the year=.________

Notes

Notes

Notes

Notes

Notes

Notes

Congratulations!!!!

You made it!!!

Completed all the challenges.

Treat yourself to something nice but don't go wild and crazy.

ENJOY !!!!

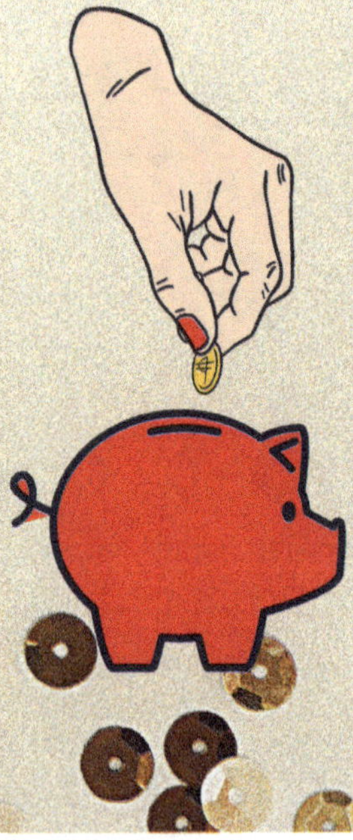

Notes

Notes

Notes

Notes

Notes

Notes

Notes

Notes

Notes

Notes

Notes

Notes

Notes

Notes

The End

"Success doesn't come from
what
you do occasionally.
It comes from what you do
consistently "

-Marie Forleo

Thank You Note

Dear Planner User,
Thank you for choosing this savings challenge planner. I hope the planner was beneficial
to your savings journey as it was to mine.
Kindly leave feedback.

Dede Sooyoo

Made in the USA
Monee, IL
02 November 2026

67385909R00044